NATURAL
THEOLOGY

Also by Kelly Cherry

NATURAL THEOLOGY

Poems by Kelly Cherry

Talk of mysteries!—Think of our life in nature,—daily to be shown matter, to come in contact with it,—rocks, trees, wind on our cheeks! the *solid* earth! the *actual* world! the *common sense*! *Contact*! *Contact*! *Who* are we? *where* are we?
                    —Henry David Thoreau, "Ktaadn"

LOUISIANA STATE UNIVERSITY PRESS
Baton Rouge and London
1988

Typeface: Caslon
Typesetter: G & S Typesetters, Inc.
Printer: Thomson-Shore, Inc.
Binder: John Dekker & Sons

Grateful acknowledgment is made to the following publications, in
which some of these poems originally appeared: *Abba, Anglican Theo-
logical Review, Chowder Review, Christian Science Monitor, Concern-
ing Poetry, Esquire, Georgia Review, Midwest Quarterly, New Orleans
Review, Open Places, Parnassus, Remington Review, Southern Poetry
Review, Southern Review, Sou'wester,* and *Yarrow.*

Lines from "No Particular Place to Go" by Chuck Berry © 1964,
1965 Arc Music Corp. are reprinted by permission. All rights
reserved.

Publication of this book has been supported by a grant from the
National Endowment for the Arts in Washington, D.C., a federal
agency.

Library of Congress Cataloging-in-Publication Data

Cherry, Kelly.
  Natural theology.

  I. Title.
PS3553.H357N3   1988   811'.54   87-12479
ISBN 0-8071-1430-8
ISBN 0-8071-1431-6 (pbk.)

Contents

I

Phylogenesis

She cracks her skin
like a shell, and goes in

She camps in her womb
She sucks the marrow from her bones

and sips bison's blood
in the afternoon; for years,

snow piles outside the cave she burrows in
She wakes to warm weather,

fur on her four feet, grass
rising and falling in waves like water

She feeds on flowering plants,
enjoys a cud of orchid and carrot

In the Middle Permian, scales slippery as shale appear
on her back; her spine unfurls a sail broadside

to the sun, filling with a light like wind, while *Sphenodon*
turns its third eye on the sky, sensing

rain, and rock salt washes into the ocean
Silent as mist, she slides down a mud bank on her underbelly

Lobe-finned and fleshy,
she pumps air through her gills

She's soft as jelly
Her skull is limestone

She drifts, like a continent
or a protozoan, on the planet's surface,

and sinks into the past
like a pebble into a brackish pool

The seas catch fire
The earth splits and gapes

The earth cracks open like an egg
and she goes in

We begin

When the Earth Slept Under Snow, and Its Dreams Were of Diamond

There was a time when the earth slept
Under snow, and its dreams were of diamond
And oil, or under the blank-browed summer sky,
And its dreams were unchanged because the dreams
Were change. Then came a day, shortly before the beginning
Of history, when I wandered into an autumn forest
With a hard floor, and saw you sitting on a felled log,
The still light filtering through the leaves of trees
With a quiet fineness like that of dark red roses
Or goldfish. I was lost, or I was found,
Sunk in that moment. There must have been sound
But memory has lacquered the skylark's song,
The raccoon at the river, the darning-needle's noisy nosedives,
The kingfisher hitting water, the constant
Steady slippage of things from their place.
I remember only a burnished, glowing silence
And the way you touched me. After that,
Nothing was the same. Or rather, everything was the same—
Nothing ever changed, because the only center was you, and
    without you,
There could not even be said to have been change
Because nothing would exist by which to measure change.
So nothing changed, and cities grew up and fell down,
Frenzied or weary, and people were born and died,
And the countries' boundaries were different colors
According to the leaders' maps, and all this time
I was with you, and I kissed you lovingly
While the rain ran down the gutter from the roof of the veranda
And streamed in the mud by the side of the house, flattening
The long grass. The lime trees grew green and lush.
The lime trees grew green and lush, but at last the leaders,
Sensing they lacked control over certain of their citizens,
Built a bomb. A fireplant. They came at night when ordinary
    people
Might be expected to be in bed, and they took you away
In a warhead. Today I live uncaressed in a cement building
With cracked outside walls, where weeds busy themselves
Climbing, poking their fibrous fingers into poured rock.

In the parking lot, dead cars broil in the sun like tin chickens
Trussed with wire. Did the earth dream this?
The breeze lifts the white silk curtain of my window, and I know
That this dust sifting over the glossy deep blue sill
Is earth I walked on, centuries ago,
And though nothing has changed, everything has changed,
And we are all of us doomed henceforth to an eternal wakefulness,
Watching our neighbors and the sky, the cloud
That may not be a cloud, the sun that may not be a sun,
Waiting, and listening to the dull banging of the hammer
As they drive the nails into our planet's free, nonpartisan heart.

Where Fire Went

In the beginning,
earth resembled hell:
Its mass seethed like an aquarium of mealworms,
and fire fell

from heaven.
Then a cloud of sulphur
moved over the face
of the earth, and in its place

came the cooling breath
of ozone, and air,
and primitive forms of death.
Everywhere,

rock became rock,
wood and water sprang
into solid existence,
and one day a bird sang.

The fire retreated;
it went underground
but was never wholly defeated.
It took new forms—

uranium, plutonium.
Some fire hid in an atom,
and some rested lazily at the planet's core,
like tinder, marking time,

knowing what it waits for.

Paranoia

You're meat and salt,
nine-tenths water; you live on a rock,
craning your neck

to see; you have always felt
something was watching you.
When you wheeled around, birds flew

off, their thin wings tipped with gilt.
Silence blistered the air
like a brush fire.

A snake began to molt
under your heel, full of spite,
while your heart beat

furiously, widening along its longest fault
like California. Now you let it go—
you know

something unseen waits in the green forest,
impersonal and persistent as moss,
hungry as a stalking beast.

The Family

The father has been killed in an accident during a hunting expedition.

The Mother Speaks

The day they came home without you,
I was teaching Mara to thread the bone needle:
chew leather, I said, the way a giraffe chews grass.

Mara's teeth are strong,
her smile is strong;
she has long lashes.

I teach my daughter the art of survival,
the home-keeping art: sweep spider webs away,
pick the twigs up from the hearth, pray.

Keep a sharp lookout: light is a snake
the color of cream, coiled
in the crotch of a tree; it spits

poison in your eye and you die.

The Brother, a Cripple, Speaks

I was doing my tricks
for the children, beating sticks
with sticks, singing a song
on one note like a bird
with one word: "Me, me, me."

My legs are air but I can't fly.
I sit in the shade of a tree,
plucking my weedy knee.
The children turn somersaults;
sun sticks to their hair like bits of straw.

I used to hunt boar,
my spear tipped with blood,

mud on my back and arms,
a necklace of sworn charms
painted across my breast

with a brush dipped in dung.
I used to hunt elephant. . . .
Elephants shed real tears for their dead,
and during the long drought I once saw a bull cry
silently, as his calves choked on yellow dust like lye.

Children: water the earth with your eye.

The Son Speaks

I remember the air was dry
as earth in summer,
or a cake of wheat baked in ashes—
but my bones were cold;
they froze in my flesh like icicles.

Mother was teaching Mara to sew.
My uncle dozed under the sycamore.

* * *

I have a dog;
his vest is white,
his feet are white;
at night, he curls by the fire,
and his hind legs jerk
in his sleep; does he dream
of chasing rabbits, squirrels?
And you—do you dream?

Uncle says dreamless sleep
is the darkest. I keep
my eyes open,
I prop my lids with my fingers
and prick my skin with the quill
of a porcupine, I swallow sand
so I won't sleep.

All night I walk
to and fro in our cave.
I leave my handprint
on the walls of our cave.
I draw the great deer
on the walls of our cave.
Firelight burns color
into the walls—
red and yellow,
the shape of shadow.
The walls of our cave
secrete beads of moisture;
I will wear a necklace of cold water.

* * *

An extravagance:
my sister will wear earrings
of raindrops.

* * *

Her eyes are as blue as the pool
at the lip of a waterfall
at twilight;
I swim in them
like a fish,
I dive down to dark.
I nap in a bed
of mud and silt
on the floor of my sister's eyes;
I rise on a sun-warmed current
to air, where forsythia
hangs over the bank in bright clumps,
like clumps of light,
dripping petals like water.

I am a willow
growing beside the pool
of my sister's gaze.
My roots sip her sweet springs
and drain her dry.

I weep with my sister's eye.

All That Mara Knows

These are the lessons I have learned by heart: give mandrake
for deep sleep, willow bark for headache;
to chase away nightmares, take
the peony's seeds by mouth.

If your man leaves you, go south.

If food is scarce, feed
on your own tongue;
what words bleed?

The celebrated stone showing my mother's form shows mine:
my stomach is lava,
my breasts are limestone,
my skin is like mica.

My hair is as red as an August poppy—

These lessons I have learned,
but I don't know why I'm loved.
Why am I loved?

My brother sleeps with his head on my shoulder;
my uncle has no legs, but he walks beside me like the wind,
embracing me as a strong wind embraces a tree.

They teach me to dig under the boulder for grubworms and mice;
they teach me where to find wild rice.

I am the best student,
the student of surpassing brilliance;
I am the first genius.
I live among the cold rocks,
tending our small fire,
cooking bear and deer.
I am learning history
by watching others die.

I know where our souls fly after death:
to the dark shelf that oozes wet salt
at the rear of the cave,
where my father's blind spirit hangs upside down
and harks to the echo
of its own thin cry.

Mara Speaks

I was sewing a shirt of animal skins,
when the hunters returned.
This is the lesson I learned:
the dead are buried sitting up;
the living lie down with one another,
uncle, mother, brother.

Hunting: A Story

I

We headed north,
summer at our backs,
living on roots and water,
following the unmistakable tracks
of the elk, as they advanced our party
day after day, all of us weary,
the Giant-winged Moth
gleaming on the oak's
breeze-blown leaves, the river
green and sparkling, liquid jewels,
the sun in it like a fish with a million flashing fins.

I forget why we had come.
It had something to do with food,
something to do with a child who died.

I could smell your shoulder at my side,
could lick salt from your arm.
At night, in the wood,
I slept wrapped in your arms
like a cob in its husk,
like a plant
breathing only the air you breathed out in your dreams,
a man's musk,
thinking, *Want*—
until you heard what I couldn't say
and answered me, kissing.

II

Our bodies' fire: the quick
spark of desire in the dark,

leaping like deer or silver trout
to the hole at the top, and out—

I warm my hands in the hollow space
between your neck and the ground's hard face,

or in the hair on your back
like a mane, and the black

night erupts into flame in our brilliant tent:
your flesh igniting mine like a flint.

III

Morning.
I fed you berries and bark.
Oh, I remember your hand on my arm
like the sun on a branch,
your eyes like hunting knives!

There was weather:
a smell of rain on the wind,
clouds racing like a herd of antelope,
thunder . . .
leaves clattering like horses' hooves on limestone.
The ground was as hard as bone,
and the sky black as a crow feather.

Don't go,
don't go.

I was hitting you
because the only words were in my fists,
I spoke them on your chest,
but you held my wrists
with one hand, and with the other drew
a ring around my breast,
thinking—what were you thinking?

I watched you go.

IV

The V of the geese
is like the dent at the base of your throat.
Their rain-color is the color of your eyes.
I am in love with geese.
I go looking for geese,
spend my long days in marshes and swamps,
scanning the sky for geese.
I dream that I am sleeping
in your wide black-fringed white wings,
and your hot, enthusiastic heart beats under my ear
but it is only the river
running,
far off, the sound rolling underground.
He-Who-Drums-Has-Drowned.

V

Winter.
The light hard as ice,
frozen between the wind-pumiced branches
like blue water between chestnut shoots,
still and solid,
the sky like a lake . . .

Winter.
I am thinking a question.
It lies curled in my brain,
waiting to be born:
sons and daughters will spring
from my mouth, I will be called
Mother-of-Many-Words. . . .

The question ends in a loop like a lasso.
Or: it is a question like a fever,
hot to the touch,
cold inside.

I shiver.

I feel the wind that is like a warrior
marking a path in the sides of trees
cutting into my legs,
and I think: I will bleed ice crystals,
there will be nothing between my legs,
only coldness and cutting.

—*But why?*

VI

Years go by—

The north wind whispers
under the mud hut walls,
it tongues my ear.
What I can't say,
only wind can hear.

There was a word once
danced in my body
sang through my throat
lived in my brain
saying itself
over and over: *you.*

The word went away,
leaving only the sound of the wind,
lonesome, mocking, sneak-sound,
old Eavesdropper, old Tattletale,
old Snake in the Grass,
wind.

VII

Now I live
like an animal,
where it is March
and April forever,
where the white sun's arch
and fall

are both so thin that noon never
quits, and dawn and dusk arrive
unannounced, mere
light dustings of shadow
on the day's long year.

VIII

Snow geese, blue geese, the greylag . . .

One by one,
shadows are peeled from the sycamore,
from the counsel-holding evergreen.

Now the pond's surface ripples
with a swift paddling of wings like oars.
Light-sweetened air, cool
as melting snow on the tongue,
drops over the still-hard ground.
Touch-me-not springs.

And when wet snow stipples
dark bark, poetry pours
from the sky, forming a pool
I wade out in, sung
to by the wind, water-kissed, hugged, and drowned.
Wind in the water's locks sings.

Sings: *The day's long year, blue snow,*
the gray geese, pale light, the evergreen
secretive as snow, the blue lag
between then and now, rippling . . .

Sings these same things,
for nothing ever really happened
but comings and goings,

comings and goings,

and goings again, until
not even that happened
and love was still

as a stone. O love (if anyone reads),
here is my heart,
trapped among snow-tipped reeds.

A Scientific Expedition in Siberia, 1913

From the log

Week One: our expedition slowed,
    Faltered, stopped; we set up
Camp and dug in, but still it snowed
    And snowed, without letup,

Until we thought we'd go insane.
    We literally lost our sense
Of balance, because sky and plain
    Were one omnipresence,

So dazzling white it could blind a man
    Or mesmerize his soul.
We lost sight of the horizon.
    There was one man, a Pole

Named Szymanowski, an expert on plants
    Of the early Pleistocene
Period, who dreamed of giants
    In the earth, swearing he'd seen

Them grow from snow like plants from dirt.
    We said that such dreams were
The price one pays for being expert,
    And laughed, but still he swore,

And still it snowed. The second week
    The ceaseless rush of wind
Was in our heads like ancient Greek,
    A curse upon our kind,

Or say: in our skulls like the drone
    Of bees swarming in a hive.
And we began to know that none,
    Or few, of us would survive.

Secretly, we sought the first signs
    Of sickness in each other,

Reading between the face's lines
        As a spy reads a letter,

But no one complained of fever,
        And suddenly the snow
Quit. You couldn't have proved it ever
        Fell, but for the wild show

Of evidence on the ground. Now
        The lid was lifted, and
Sun set icicled trees aglow
        With flame, a blue sky spanned

The hemisphere, and while we packed
        Our gear, we found we were
Singing, but Szymanowski backed
        Out, silent as the fur

On a fox . . . or the wolfish cur,
        Slinking like a shadow,
That stuck to our pack dogs like a burr.
        Where S. went, God may know,

But we went on to a frozen hill,
        A vast block of the past—
An ice cube for a drink in hell
        (If anything cools that thirst).

Inside, preserved like a foetus
        In formaldehyde, like
Life itself, staring back at us
        The mammoth creature struck

Poses for our cameras; then
        We got busy, and went
To work, and all seemed well for ten
        Days, and then some strange scent,

Not unpleasant, weighted the air,
        Sweet as fruit, and one dog
Stirred, and then another, and where
        I sat, keeping this log,

A steady dripping started up,
     Slowly at first, and then
Faster. I made my palms a cup
     To catch the flow, and when

I lapped the melted snow, I glanced
     Down, and saw how cold
Ground under my boot moved and danced
     In little streams: an old

Fear shook me and I ran to where
     The mammoth stood—freed from
Time and vulnerable to air.
     His curling tusks seemed some

Incredible extravagance,
     A creator's last spree.
His fixed stare held me in a trance,
     His reddish-brown, shaggy

Coat caught the sun like burnished oak,
     But he didn't move: was still
As if he'd been carved from a rock.
     Nothing supernatural

Was going to happen, and I breathed—
     Fresh meat on the hoof!—In
An instant, the pack dogs had covered
     Him like hungry ants spreading

Over a hatching egg, tearing
     Chunks of raw flesh from his side,
Snarling, snapping their jaws, baring
     Fangs that ripped his flank wide

Open. My hands, my boots were spattered
     With blood, and the dogs ate
Him up. That horror performed, we scattered
     Into the world, but late

In the afternoon, I saw a shadow
     At my heel, and I knew

The others were dead—numbed into slow
    Motion, and each a statue

Buried in ice. And then the clouds,
    Piled in the north and east
Like a funeral parlor's stack of shrouds,
    Darkened, sliding southwest,

And it snowed and has never stopped
    Snowing since, and I have
Come with blood in my mouth, my hands sopped
    With red snow, to speak and save.

For my father,
in memoriam

Riding the Wheel into the Center

So a wheel spins around, forward or back?
Consider
the wheel without a track.

It opens like a rubber band, or
tightens,
like a noose around your neck.

Just try to breathe.
That cord cuts into your paper throat,
and some word lies strangled there.

Senseless is the way
we die, biting tarmac and clay, going nowhere
fast, not forward or back,

riding
a wheel without a track.

Poem of the Secondhand Volkswagen

The cassette of the cardinal
creates Spring
on the front seat of your automobile.
Reading street signs by your side, I sing
in secret: no direction is impossible

to those who keep the dark in back.
Your car will now grow sunflowers
from its gray hood and shine like the black
unpaved earth each genesis explores.
At crack

of dawn let us till moving metal
into ground,
plant speed; hearing a bird call,
hope returns and turns around.
We forget the Fall.

Two Roses

She is an angel in rose
Etched on a November sky.
He is a rose—
They are two roses, burning brightly.

They kiss in the car,
Their lips like petals: pink.
They must drive far
To find God, I think.

I think that angels' wings spread
Against the sky are red
As roses, and fly not at all.
They fall

And fall, flower-flames,
And as they fall, they love and kiss,
Calling each other's cherished name.
God loves this.

God loves this—
The twining, the arc.
They fall together,
Lightly, into the winter dark.

Late Afternoon at the Arboretum

Riding along in my automobile,
My baby beside me at the wheel . . .
                —Chuck Berry

The lilacs are in bloom
and the lake that was ice
is water green as crème
de menthe. Flowering Scotch broom

tugs at the eye, Yellow
Brick Road—style. I hold
your hand; your hands, the wheel . . . .
Are we saying hello,

good-bye, something in between?
The car is a Pontiac
station wagon; it's parked
in a very pastoral scene,

and as the sun enflames
the flowers, and the sky
above the arboretum
flares, then dims, making the names

of the trees difficult
to read, I study your face
in profile, now thinking
what dear Ruth had said, exult-

ing in her conscience, to
Naomi: Wherever
you go, I will come along.
        Here amid the alien heather
        and words from an old song,
I say her words, to you.

Used

The mind-body problem

My mind grows cold
and sluggish. No antifreeze salesman
will ever rev her up again.
She's too old

for new parts.
She stands in an empty lot
remembering those bright, false starts
everyone else forgot

so quickly.
As snow packs in around the wheels,
she becomes her abandoned body,
knows how it feels

to reflect the winter sun
in the dent on the door
she will not open
anymore.

Volga Car Song

When the KGB come after you,
>it's in a white Volga with a fake license
plate: an "operational vehicle."

The black limousines are reserved
>for party bosses. Silent as eels, they slip
into side streets marked NO ENTRANCE,

but the white Volga stays with you
>always—it is your shadow, or a
photographer's negative of a shadow, and it
comes with you all the way to the cemetery
at midnight in the dead, as it were, of
winter,

where it parks just out of sight.
>The willow of strength and the willow
of sorrow at the far end glitter like ice
sculpture,

but you stand by the small square,
>crunching snow underfoot and warming
your hands by the memorial torch,

and the KGB run their motor,
>idling. Do they smoke American cigarettes?
Drink vodka from a fliptop bottle? Do they
dream of being at home and in bed or even
just in bed?

The life of a KGB agent is a hard one,
>God knows. Paperwork all day, and at
night—shadowing lovers to the cemetery.
Oh,

it's work and no thanks,
>except an occasional bribe (special discount
stores, schools, doctors, imported goods,

travel abroad, dachas, and free girls at the
unpublicized resort outside Moscow).

But is it *worth* it, Boris,
that ache in the joints, the wind seeping in
around the edges of the window, that stink
of petrol, rubber and snow shoved in your
face like a hand, that gag, that lifelong gag
around the bought mouth?

Heading back to town, we wave;
the white Volga rolls out of the pines
slowly, as if in search of dignity, but it lacks
autonomy—it can't go anywhere without
our lead. We are pulling all Russia around
by the nose; left to itself, it can only
dematerialize,

vanishing, like Amelia Earhart, into the morning mist.

III

The Rose

A botanical lecture

It's the cup of blood,
the dark drink lovers sip,
the secret food

It's the pulse and elation
of girls on their birthdays,
it's good-byes at the railroad station

It's the murmur of rain,
the blink of daylight
in a still garden, the clink
of crystal; later, the train

pulling out, the white cloth,
apples, pears, and champagne—
good-bye! good-bye!
We'll weep petals, and dry
our tears with thorns

A steep country springs up beyond
the window, with a sky like a pond,

a flood. It's a rush
of bright horror, a burning bush,
night's heart,
the living side of the holy rood

It's the whisper of grace in the martyrs' wood

Natural Theology

You read it in the blue wind,
the blue water, the rock spill,
the blue hill

rising like a phoenix from ash. Some mind
makes itself known through the markings of light
on air; where earth rolls, right

comes after, our planet's bright spoor. . . . If you look, you'll find
truth etched on the tree trunk,
the shark's tooth, a shell, a hunk

of root and soil. Study from beginning to end.
Alpha and omega—these are the cirrus alphabet,
the Gnostics' cloudy "so—and yet."

If a tree falls in a forest, a scared hind
leaps, hearing branches break;
you crawl under the log and shake

honey out of a hollow, eggs from a nest, ants from the end
of a stick; resting, you read God's name on the back of a bass
in a blue pool; God grows everywhere, like grass.

Heartwood: A Diary

Stouter ones hold heartwood at the centre.
                    —*The Observer's Book of Trees*

The secret lies in the winter-resting buds
and *cambium*, a tissue one cell thick.
Or, what makes trees tick?

Consider conifers,
the broad-leaved beech and ash,
the oak on Auclum Close,
how light rests on their branches
like birds' nests—out of reach,
full of flight.

November 1st.
Night. Write:
Lichen lives on a knob of bark.
A tree is a growing stick.
These truths are a way to knowing dark.

February. It's snowing.
All day I sit at my desk.
At four o'clock the snow stops,
the wind stops, the world stops,
and I go out to gaze on my shadow,
cool as meltwater.

The weeks unwind, like a ribbon unfurled.

Spring moves north
at the rate of sixteen miles a day,
a green clay.
Shape into leaves, grass;
fire and glaze.
These are the *ways* of the world:
to dig and plant, bake in the sun.

All things come to fruition.

How to Wait

First things first: dig in at the lake's edge.
Use sedge for your rug;
sleep on a stone ledge.

No phonographs needed here—
the music you hear is made by a dozen soft tongues
lapping water, by a hungry lion,
deer.

Sun brands your shoulders;
you are singled out for life
by this indelible contact.

Yes, you might as well face facts.
The eyes see you,
the men pity you.
The animals would like to devour you.
No one will save you.

You live by the lake, waiting.
Things to do:

For supper, suck the meat
from a crayfish, or chew watery plants,
spitting out what you can't eat—
it'll feed the white ants
fumbling at your feet.

When the moon comes up, look by its light
for changes—the mountains that move
nearer, the sky that drops,
trees that shed their bark and grow into giants overnight—

The next day, rain.

Locate a thicket to hide in.
Before you enter, make sure it's empty.
That commotion? A cricket.

All day you wait.

You are so damp that beans sprout from your skin,
flowers from your fingertips.
You are budding; open
your mouth to fate
and take it in—
those lips are already smeary with sin.

Generously flick seeds aside.

Grow in the ground; become one
with earth and sun.

Surrender yourself. Evaporate. Abide.

My Calendar

The day of longing, when light
loses itself among the serpentine vines and brambles,
reflecting

The day of the string quartet:
that music's with me yet,
pure as spring water;
I fish in it with my net of words

The day I lay in someone's arms,
listening to the clock tick—
outside, it was dusk;
down the hall, someone was cooking cabbage for supper

The day of death,
its breath soft as chinchilla against your skin

Always, I celebrate the day
of newness, clover and lilies,
when air smells sweet as talc,
the grass glows,
and shadow is rolled away like a stone from the door of a sepulcher

Forecast

The bombs are not falling yet—
Only snow, wet snow, thick snow. Storybook snow.
Yet like most of us, I keep waiting for the bombs.
We know that one day the weatherman will say,
Good morning, America! Dress warmly.
Stay indoors if you can. Try not to drive.
And now for the outlook. Observe
Our wonderful satellite photograph:
In this area, we expect a high-pressure area
Of MX missiles, and over here, to this side
Of the Rockies, something is brewing,
Something radioactive. But cheer up.
This is only the outlook. Weather is wonderful;
It can always change. For today,
Your typical air masses are cold but stable,
And the SAC umbrella remains furled
In the closet of its silos, underground bases,
And twenty-four-hour sky-watches. Today
We have snow, wet snow, thick snow. Storybook snow.
Today we are going to live happily ever after.

Lines Written on the Eve of a Birthday

It is the loss of possibility
That claims you bit by bit. They take away
Your man, the children you had hoped would be,
They even take brown hair and give you gray
Instead. You ask if you can save your face
But that is part of their plan—to strip you
Of your future and put the past in its place.
They don't stop there. They take the skies' deep blue
And drain it off; the empty bowl they leave
Inverted, white as bone. They dust the trees
With strontium, but they keep up their sleeve
The biggest trick of all, the one that sees
      You give up in the end. It is the loss
      Of possibility that murders us.

Night Air

A pavane

These are the nights of being inner-isolated,
dangerous nights when the bed
closes up like a rose, dark red

under the starlight and still moon
air. Nights when no one
can breathe. The cold horn

spills its notes across the sky,
flings them ruthlessly
to the ground, saying: Someone someone knows is going to die.

Oh yes, the moist air clings to the cave of the throat
like a bat,
and won't fly. Last night, tonight,

a cloud dimmed the eye of God,
like a cataract. The bed,
too, the bed is becoming blind,

is closing,
cradling
Satan's seed, the iris-corroding devil's drop, dew, is becoming

forgotten and heart-
sick, set apart,

is becoming you.

The Lonely Music

My name is Calliope but some call me Pain,
pronounced like "rain."

I am the lonely music.
I curl on the blue floor like a cat.
I spring from your heart like blood.
The cut flowers echo your mood—

They make a fist and punch air
but I kiss your ear,
knock on wood—
Are you glad I came?

The lonely music lives in you
like a person in a room,
and enters and leaves and returns,
telling you all that she learns:

The touch of a wet leaf, cool
as the scaffolding of a batwing.
In the school of sense, students sing
low notes in the key of grief.

You are the star there, the one who knows
my name: Despair.

I am the music that comes and goes.

Your Going Out

To my mother

I do not think I can bear
this: your going out,
ray by ray, being swallowed up
in shadow, until I can hardly make out

your form in the world.
Your long-distance voice
is both a reassurance and a threat,
love, and pain, an absence met—

I listen to its eager, faint, girlish, southern accent
and think: I do not think
I can bear
this: your letters, each sent,

diminishing like a chord, the fact
that you have had to give up playing
the violin, which was always what you loved best,
next to Father. I do not think I can bear *that*—

his need for you
having to go unanswered despite your willingness,
his desperate hoping,
hoping,

that your silence means only he is growing
deaf,
or this: knowing
that not all our love can keep you

as you have been, shining,
and comic and pure,
your fine energy
that compels us to endure.

Ithaca

I remember a hall of doors
opening and closing. Goldfish
nibbled grainy bits in a glass bowl,
and sunlight stained the walls and floor
like finger paint. I remember
the silence, thick and spongy as bread,
and sound cutting through it like a knife.
Oh, I remember my life then, how
my parents played their violins
half the night, rehearsing, while snow
piled on the sill outside the pane.
Mike was making a model plane;
the baby slept, sucking her thumb.
I used to come home from school late—
detained for misbehavior, or
lost in a reverie on State
Street: *I, Odysseus, having dared*
to hear the sirens' song, my ears
unstopped, have sailed to Ithaca,
where the past survives. Last of all,
I remember dressing for school;
it was still dark outside, but when
the sun rose, it melted the snow.
My galoshes had small brass clasps.

Plans for a House in Latvia

In a basket on the sideboard,
pile ripe apples;
when the sun reaches them through the open door,
we'll have fire for food.

In fine weather, you write music out back—
or steal off.
"Good fishing among birches and pines!"

In the winter, we skate
on the lake in the field,
and come in late,
blowing on our hands.

Silence falls on the little house,
sticking like snow all around,
the only sound your voice,
startling and mysterious
as the shadow of a blue spruce
cast across cold ground.

At night, Princess leaps from the wood floor
to the chair where she sleeps,
while we share the big bed.

Your warm body covers mine like a blanket.

Dear heart,
a final note about the kitchen.
Keep the teacups Pēteris painted
on a safe shelf:
one is for love,
one is for faith's long-enduring self.

At Night Your Mouth

At night your mouth moved over me
Like a fox over the earth, skimming
Light and low over the rising surfaces of my body,
Hugging the horizon against hunters;
Or like the other hunted, the one who runs
Back exposed like a billboard to the barbed wire and starved dogs,
The men in guard towers, danger sweeping the snow-patched yard
Every thirty seconds, the shirt you tore,
To make a tourniquet for your leg, fluttering like a signpost
Against the branch of a birch tree, saying THIS WAY:
You were looking for someplace to hide, to crawl into,
A place to lie down in and breathe
Or not-breathe until the dogs pulled the hunters past,
Fooled by water, wind, snow, or sheer luck,
And I folded myself around you like a hill and a valley,
And the stars in my hair shone only for you,
Combed into cold blue and deep red lights,
And the river ran warm as blood under its lid of ice,
And my throat was like an eel pulsing between your palms,
And the air in my blood was tropical, I caught my breath
And held it between my teeth for you
To eat like a root,
There were black grouse in the forest
And the moon on the snow was as gold as your skin
As I remember it shining on Nightingale Lane,
But the dogs' barking in the distance carried too clearly,
A man snapped, STĀT!
And you trembled, troubled and impassioned,
You covered your eyes with your hand,
And I felt the shudder slam like the sea
Pummeled by God's fist,
Wind-bit waves sizzling against the fiery cliffs of Liepāja—
And you were the ship
The harbor dreams of, the brave husband
The bride awaits, the seed
For which the earth has prepared itself with minerals and salts,
And I folded myself around you like a windrow and a furrow,
And whispered, so no one, not dog or man or man-dog, would
    overhear: *Now*
Now now now
Escape into me.

47

Letter to a Censor

Simply, one must imagine what has been lost:
The light along the edge of the lake gone dark

As death, leftover leaves
Crumbled into mulch and ground

Underfoot, a cry
Like a bird's or a child's, imprinting the waxsoft sky

With its echo, mind with memory—
Lost, lost. One must imagine

What has been, what has been lost
Between the third line and the fifth

Between the first page and the third
Between the third envelope and the fifth

With its official *Recommandé*.
And night eats up the flowers of the day.

One must imagine what has been
Lost in the mouth of the censor

Swallowed
Shat from the bowels of the censor

And lost. Lost. Perhaps one lives somewhere which is not
Where the one whom that one loves lives,

And then one must imagine the shortest distance
Between these two points

A line,
Deleted.

Perhaps one whom one has loved in August
Is forbidden to write in November, and his words appear at night

Like stars in the dome of the brain's planetarium.
Or perhaps it is still later, and the scene shifts

As scenes do,
Wordlessly.

The mind drops heavily into sleep, the undersides of the lids
Are painted with bright, moving pictures—

We are dancing a minuet in the mind.
The great gate strains against its lock in the noisy night wind.

The lake's blackness is rolling over and under its winking
    whiteness
And the lights in the mansion glow like white-gold winter stars.

Simply, there is a storm picking up and strewing all things before
    it like confetti
And words are scattered into silence like frightened animals, lost,

And love and friendship are separated, lost,
Summer has become the orphan of the seasons, abandoned, lost,

And music is drowned on the wind.

We are dancing a minuet in the mind.
One must imagine.

Prayer for a Future Beyond Ideology and War

When the world dissolves in its own chemicals
And the people's bodies are as ghostly as the particles discovered by
    Josephson in 1962, which pass through walls like light through
    air,
And the people's buildings are born again as blueprints, and the
    print is invisible and the blue is the blue of the innocent,
    amnesiac sea,
And the hardwood trees, falling in forests everywhere, their
    fractured branches tangled like a woman's hair after love, make
    no sound not because they are not heard but because there is no
    longer anything for them to land on and thud against
(The pine trees like unplayed whole notes trapped in a barbed-wire
    stave)—

And even the stones have become as insubstantial as thought—

May there be new cities in the tolerant sky,
Held in place by their own gravity
(Or lack of it), places of peace where a man and a woman
Holding each other in the familiar bed of their long night
May see, through the window, as clear as light
The stubbornly loving shadow of a star that was once our sun.

IV

Questions and Answers

In the beginning was the Word . . .
—John 1 : 1

And about the ninth hour Jesus cried
with a loud voice, saying, Eli, Eli,
lama sabachthani? that is to say, My
God, my God, why hast thou forsaken me?
—Matthew 27 : 46

In the beginning is the beginning
And all beginnings, points of darkness becoming
Points of light, the pulsing dot of yellow
Or red or blue shimmering in the space
Where a soul is about to create itself
Out of the surrounding unnameable
Nothingness. After this stage you can expect
A great silence to descend, like a cloth
Dropping over the smooth top of a mahogany table, forever.
This silence is the way you felt when you were a child
And counted inwardly for three days, stopping only to eat,
Holding your breath as the numbers mounted higher
And higher and seemed as if they would surely topple
Like a tower of blocks, trying to reach
Infinity. Or when you stared at the electric clock
(The one with Roman numerals on the kitchen wall),
And you fought back the desire to blink, desperate to catch the
    minute hand
At the moment of its fatal jumping. All this failure
Lies in a heap on the floor of your heart,
Scooters with one wheel, blind Teddy bears,
Chinese checkers with two colors incomplete in their triangles,
The new puppy dead on German School Road.
There is always that: the hole in the side
Of eternity, through which time leaks into the world,
A plasmic spatter, heart's blood on the hillside,
Running off into the gullies like the rain
Which is said to have been as dark as ink.
They used to make a fountain pen that was transparent,
So you could see when you needed to fill it again.
Torn pages: you will go to the library and find
That in every book you take down from the shelf
A page has been removed by someone who has

Preceded you in the night, and it was precisely
The page for which you were looking, your hand trembling
As you turned to the table of contents. *I always knew,*
She says, *it was ridiculous to say a thing*
Like that. Here we will be sorrowful, bitter,
Sardonic, and the light that flashes in the brain
Like the blue light on a patrol car will turn and turn,
Looking down alleys lined with garbage cans,
While rain soaks into the cop's pants legs and he curses
Somebody, the night, the anonymous tip, you.
There are mini-rainbows in the oil-slick puddles, luminous
Under the cloud-streaked moon. You have made a mental portrait,
Pieced from photographs, of her face, her impassive eyes,
Her bleached blonde hair, pale white as the pulp of an apple,
And the question is, How are we to step outside
Of all these likenesses and dissimilarities
Which surround us like a container with no outside?
Did *he* glance startled back at the one who had suddenly
    recognized him,
Disbelieving that the reflection could be greater than the thing
    reflected?
Did the anxiety in his heart presage an instant when love
Would spin away, screwing itself like a tornado
To a vanishing point, leaving only
The vertigo of despair, the giddy view downward to hell,
Or was it merely the consequence, the scar, of discovering he
    had been
From the beginning one who would come after, always after,
A feeling as when you sat in study hall
And carefully pulled against the closing of your notebook's three
    rings
At the same time you released the spring, but the snap,
When it came, was too loud anyway, and you made a face
As if to disassociate yourself from the event.
You must answer this question. You do not have
All the time in the world. The shadow of the dove
Is flickering on the concrete pillar. A bird
Like a brushstroke is swerving idiosyncratically
Or along unseen lines, dipping
In and out of sight over the sailboat
And glittering water. Have you thought how it will be
When you are no longer present at this window,

And the autumn leaves turn red and yellow
And loosen and swoop and hang-glide even without
You to watch them? The squirrel collecting acorns,
The hiker rounding a curve—what will not go on? You may become
Resigned or angry, thinking about this.
What is inevitable is that you should recall
With a clarity so intense that it seems astonishing
In spite of its inevitability
The expression on the face of one man
Whom you have loved for so long that loving him and being you
Appear to be the same, that loving him
May even be what called you into existence
In the first place, so that who you are, is
An afterthought, but inescapable.
You heard someone saying your name
In the night, and woke with a start,
Blinking at the sound which threaded its way
Into your brain and heart like Beethoven's
Music, feeling created and new. His hands
Covered your face and in the darkness of his palms
You lived a million years, every day
Of which was like an emerald and a ruby.
What does this mean? What does it mean? What?
That there are portents if you look for them?
This is not a question, and the only possible answer to it
Is ambiguous. For the sake of the poem, it is
September in Wisconsin, becoming October,
And the colors are blue and gold and green, with white
Clouds which, if the day were colder, you might imagine
Were made by God's breath, the Hidden One revealing his
   presence
In the divine huff, if you believed in God and were not,
As you are, called upon to perform these actions
In a variety of moods, all unanchored by any confirmation.
You know only that you have been abandoned
Among twigs, pebbles, grasses, hubcaps, and bits
Of broken bottle glass, and the thing you must accomplish,
After your friends have been picked off one by one
By the sniper in the radio tower and dusk has settled
Over the construction site, a few shreds of light snagged
On the barbed-wire fence, like pieces of caught cloth, is
Forgiveness. This is the hard part. This is the feeling

You were chasing down corridors, the feeling you were seeking to
  capture
When you sank the dragnet into your mind's depths
And came up with everything but. Here we are thinking of
Rejection slips, the KGB, murder.
A man has been nailed to some sticks of wood
And his insides are sagging into his bowels.
Time is swirling around the sparse weeds, eroding
And seeping into the sandy earth, and the question is,
Who is this man? There are holes in his wrists
Through which wind roars like wind in a wind tunnel,
And the sound slices into your skull like shrapnel, a fragment
No surgeon will ever be able to excise. It will stay
With you always, that memory of how it felt,
Hanging there, pierced, and tied to the crossbeam by leather
Thongs. The bad taste in your mouth had nothing to do
With vinegar—it was knowing you had been last, and only
For this. Not the *cross;* that was to be expected.
What was insupportable—what was wholly beyond reason—
Was that you were supposed to feel no dismay about it.
No resentment. *None.* It was too much to ask.
It was like the time you looked into the mirror
And discovered that your future and your past were written there,
In minute detail, and the sole way you could revise
A single line was by slowly and painfully
Erasing yourself. Later, though you had tried,
The people were staring, they kept looking at you
And laughing, and you didn't know why, but then, in the middle
Of the crowd, you saw one man who looked at you
With such tenderness that it confused you, and you lowered your
  eyes,
Blushing, pleased. The valentine box in fifth grade,
Lace-edged, crepe-covered cardboard on which red hearts
Were pasted, heretofore charged with residual anxiety,
Has now been completely transformed by this reassurance
To an object of deep nostalgic affection! And the memories
Drift gently down around you, falling like leaves,
Until you are walking through your past, each memory
An ash of burnt air, a poker chip, a thin shaving
Of sky colored and curled. There was a turn
Here, and it has been very subtly made.
We have arrived where we can examine the situation

In its entirety. This is no elephant tusk or ear.
It is the view from all sides simultaneously,
Or, to put it another way, it is
The present status of Observatory Drive
As seen from that remembered instant long ago
When you knew you had rounded a curve
And gone on into a lifetime of longing and joy,
Though the two were not—or you, being unfond of tension,
Were not ready to accept they were—linked.
The football fans are leaning on their horns
And waving flags from tiny Buicks, and
The final question is in sight. *You will
Do this or that:* Is this declarative,
Or is it a command? *This* is the question.
You will, say, one day go into your parents' bedroom
And discover that no one has slept there for years.
If you lie on the bed, dust will rise from the spread
And sift back through the still air onto your white silk sleeves.
Was this prediction, or did someone send you there,
Someone who is not willing to show himself
Yet? This *is* the question, this *is* the question.
Things are not so simple, it seems, as certain ones
Who have gone before us have suggested:
There are implications everywhere,
Whispering in the tops of trees, urgent,
Restless, waiting, darting across the ground
Just a second before you turn your head,
So you never quite see them, just their shadows,
The light stabilizing itself after the sudden disturbance.
Today's sun has moved on to California, leaving behind
A rose sky that flattens out over the lake, widening into darkness
And deep blue ripples. And now the far shore is gone,
Vanished, the island is bleeding into the margin,
And here on the bank the reeds rustle uneasily
In a rising wind, the shed feathers of forgotten sparrows
Are stirred, ruffled, and dropped, a large rat
Slips into the water—does he touch your foot?
You are surrounded by unseen eyes in the dark,
And the wind has snuffed out the fire in your tin box.
And there are sounds in the forest, there are coals in the
    campsite pit
Not from your pack, still warm, warm as a baby's breath,

And you know that the others, the ones who were
Here first, are now hiding not far, only
Outside the rim, in the woods beyond the cleared place,
Whispering. *Come,* say the voices, *come with us.*
For you will, you know. And they say:
We will go into the unknown together,
Drawing the long sentence of ourselves after us,
Until only the tip end of it is visible,
A bit of blackness, a point, like a period.